YOUR ANCIENT GREECE

Homework Helper

by John D. Clare
Consultant: Dr. Christy Constantakopoulou

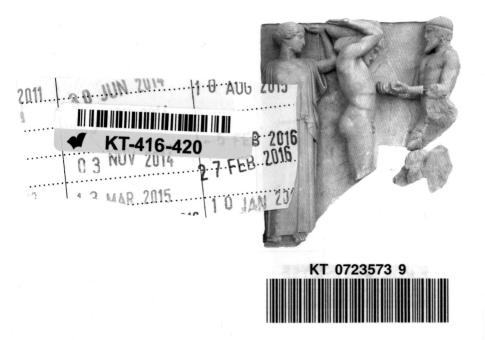

How to use this book

Each topic in this book is clearly labelled and contains all these components:

Topic heading

Introduction to the topic

Sub-topic 1 offers complete information about one aspect of the topic

Choose a word from the Keyword Contents on page 3. Then, turn to the correct page and look for your word in BOLD CAPITALS. This will take you straight to the information you need

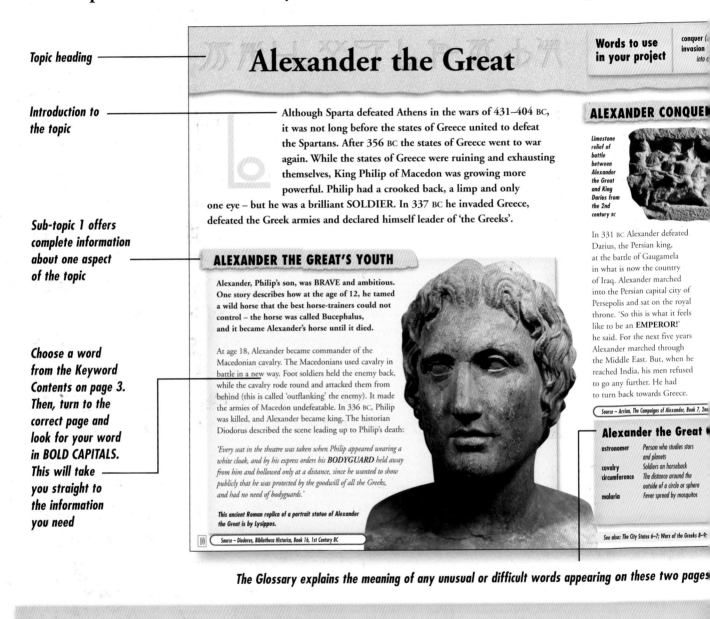

Alexander the Great

Words to use in your project — conquer, invasion, into c...

Although Sparta defeated Athens in the wars of 431–404 BC, it was not long before the states of Greece united to defeat the Spartans. After 356 BC the states of Greece went to war again. While the states of Greece were ruining and exhausting themselves, King Philip of Macedon was growing more powerful. Philip had a crooked back, a limp and only one eye – but he was a brilliant SOLDIER. In 337 BC he invaded Greece, defeated the Greek armies and declared himself leader of 'the Greeks'.

ALEXANDER THE GREAT'S YOUTH

Alexander, Philip's son, was BRAVE and ambitious. One story describes how at the age of 12, he tamed a wild horse that the best horse-trainers could not control – the horse was called Bucephalus, and it became Alexander's horse until it died.

At age 18, Alexander became commander of the Macedonian cavalry. The Macedonians used cavalry in battle in a new way. Foot soldiers held the enemy back, while the cavalry rode round and attacked them from behind (this is called 'outflanking' the enemy). It made the armies of Macedon undefeatable. In 336 BC, Philip was killed, and Alexander became king. The historian Diodorus described the scene leading up to Philip's death:

'Every seat in the theatre was taken when Philip appeared wearing a white cloak, and by his express orders his BODYGUARD held away from him and hollowed only at a distance, since he wanted to show publicly that he was protected by the goodwill of all the Greeks, and had no need of bodyguards.'

This ancient Roman replica of a portrait statue of Alexander the Great is by Lysippos.

Source – Diodorus, Bibliotheca Historica, Book 16, 1st Century BC

ALEXANDER CONQUE[R...]

Limestone relief of battle between Alexander the Great and King Darius from the 2nd century BC

In 331 BC Alexander defeated Darius, the Persian king, at the battle of Gaugamela in what is now the country of Iraq. Alexander marched into the Persian capital city of Persepolis and sat on the royal throne. 'So this is what it feels like to be an **EMPEROR!**' he said. For the next five years Alexander marched through the Middle East. But, when he reached India, his men refused to go any further. He had to turn back towards Greece.

Source – Arrian, The Campaigns of Alexander, Book 7, 2n[d...]

Alexander the Great [...]

astronomer	Person who studies stars and planets
cavalry	Soldiers on horseback
circumference	The distance around the outside of a circle or sphere
malaria	Fever spread by mosquitos

See also: The City States 6–7; Wars of the Greeks 8–9;

The Glossary explains the meaning of any unusual or difficult words appearing on these two pages

Copyright © *ticktock* Entertainment Ltd 2004

First published in Great Britain in 2004 by *ticktock* Media Ltd.,

Unit 2, Orchard Business Centre, North Farm Road, Tunbridge Wells, Kent, TN2 3XF

We would like to thank: Institute of Archaeology at University College London, and Egan-Reid Ltd for their help with this book.

ISBN 1 86007 539 8 HB

ISBN 1 86007 533 9 PB

Printed in China

Sub-topic 2 offers complete information about one aspect of the topic

Some suggested words to use in your project

The Case Study is a closer look at a famous person, artefact or building that relates to the topic

knowledge *(facts or intelligence about something)*
slaughter *(killing of many people)*
tactics *(the plans of carrying out a military operation),*
usurp *(seize power)*

RE

...probably of
ome believe he
and died.
ns were
orian Arrian:

*nothing small
He would not
in satisfied
r, not even if
o Asia and the
He would always
some unknown
al himself if not*

CASE STUDY

Alexandria and Hellenism
After Alexander died, the Greeks **RULED** the Middle East for the next two centuries. The city of Alexandria in Egypt became a centre of learning, famous for its library and museum. There, the Greek astronomer Hipparchus calculated the exact length of the year, and the Greek scientist Eratosthenes calculated the circumference of the earth. The people of Alexandria built a lighthouse on the offshore island of Pharos so famous that the modern French word for **LIGHTHOUSE** is 'phare'. Strabo, writing in the 1st century BC, describes the Pharos of Alexandria:

'On top of the island there is a tower magnificently built of white stone, several storeys high, which bears the same name as the island. This was dedicated for the safety of the sailors.'

Each photo or illustration is described and discussed in its accompanying text

*f learning
rch
ound the sides of
force and attacking
behind
v of an original*

This Roman bronze coin comes from Pharos island, near Alexandria in Egypt.

Captions clearly explain what is in the picture

Source - Geography, by Strabo, 1st Century BC   11

Other pages in the book that relate to what you have read here are listed in this bar

At the bottom of each section, a reference bar tells you where the quote has come from

Keyword Contents

Ancient Greece

Ancient Greece is the name given to the country we know as modern GREECE and a civilisation of people that first lived thousands of years ago. Experts divide the history of the region into different periods: the Minoan period (3,000–1,500 BC), the Mycenaean period (about 1,700–1,100 BC), the Dark Ages period (1,100–850 BC), the Archaic period (850–480 BC), the Classical period (480–323 BC) and the Hellenistic period (323–146 BC).

LOCATION AND LANDSCAPE

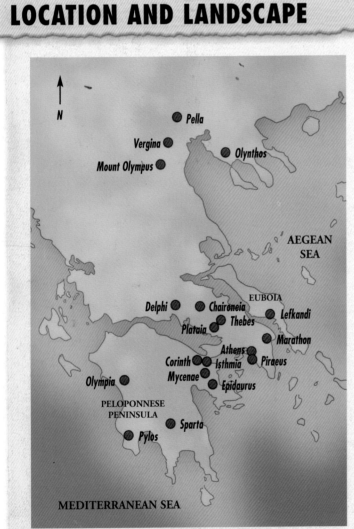

This map of ancient Greece, shows the main settlements.

Greece is a mountainous country, lying at the eastern end of the MEDITERRANEAN sea.

The **CLIMATE** is mostly hot and dry, with some light rains in winter. It was not good **FARMLAND** and Hesiod, a Greek writer from the 7th century BC, described a typical Greek farmer this way:

'... *struggling with rocks and getting nothing from the land but weeds, and aches and pains'. (1)*

The Greek writer Aristotle thought that the Greek climate made the Greeks great.

'*Those who live in a cold climate and in Europe are full of spirit, but wanting in intelligence and skill; ... the natives of Asia are intelligent and inventive, but they are wanting in spirit ... But the Hellenic race ... situated between them, is likewise intermediate in character, being high-spirited and also intelligent. Hence it continues free, and is the best-governed of any nation, and, if it could be formed into one state, would be able to rule the world.' (2)*

Source – Hesiod, Works and Days, 7th century BC (1); Aristotle, Politics, 350 BC (2)

Words to use in your project

archaeologists *(people who study history by digging up the past)*	**communities** *(groups of people living together)*	**Mediterranean** *(countries bordering the Mediterranean sea between Europe and Asia)*
arid *(hot, dry climate)*	**culture** *(customs and beliefs)*	

GREAT INVENTORS

This marble relief from the sanctuary of Amphiaros in Oropos shows a doctor giving medical treatment, 400–350 BC.

The ancient Greeks' curiosity about the way things worked led them to invent many devices and to develop many areas of knowledge that are still explored today. Examples of such areas of learning include **GEOGRAPHY**, algebra and geometry. The ancient Greeks were also the first civilisation to use theatre as a means of entertainment. The Olympic Games was another ancient Greek creation. Many modern ideas about **SCIENCE** and **MEDICINE** have their origins in ancient Greece. For example, doctors today are still sworn in as doctors by reciting 'The Hippocratic Oath' which begins like this:

'I swear by Apollo the healer, by Asclepius, by Health and all the powers of healing and call to witness all the gods and goddesses that I may keep this oath to the best of my ability and judgement.'

Source – Hippocratic corpus, c. 5th–1st centuries BC

Ancient Greece Glossary

algebra	*Type of maths that uses letters and sumbols to represent numbers*	**Hippocratic Oath**	*The oath that doctors swear, promising to try to heal the sick*
colonies	*Countries under the control of another country*	**labyrinth**	*Maze-like network of passages*
civilisation	*A people who live together in communities*	**minotaur**	*Mythical creature who is half man and half bull*
climate	*The weather conditions of an area*	**notorious**	*Famous for being bad*

CASE STUDY

The throne room of King Minos at the Palace of Knossos dating from 1,720 BC can still be seen today.

The Minoans

The Minoan civilisation existed at Knossos in Crete between 3,000 and 1,500 BC. Before it was wiped out by northern raiders, the Minoans influenced the Mycenaean culture, which began developing in northern Greece towards the end of the Minoan period. The Minoans were named after King Minos. According to legend, King Minos once lived in a huge palace in Crete. Underneath the palace was a labyrinth where a minotaur was said to live. Like the legend, the Minoans built huge maze-like palaces. The writer Thucydides wrote about King Minos:

'Minos organised a navy and sea communications improved. He sent colonies to most islands and drove out the notorious pirates, with the result that those who lived on the sea-coasts could now become wealthy and live in peace.'

Source – Thucydides, The History of the Peloponnesian War, 5th century BC

The City States

From 750 BC Greek cities and nearby villages began to form independent self-governing states. These states introduced the first form of democracy, with ordinary people involved in the making of decisions and LAWS. The Greek word for a city state was 'polis', which is where the modern word 'POLITICS' comes from. The largest polis was Athens on the coast, and Sparta, situated in an inland valley. From this time, the Greeks also began to set up colonies abroad.

RULES AND SOCIETY

In Athens, in 621 BC, a ruler named Draco introduced a set of laws which had such extreme punishments that we still use the word 'draconian' to mean a cruel law or decision. The Greek writer, Plutarch wrote this about Draco:

'For one punishment, death, was laid down for nearly all offenders, with the result that even those convicted of idleness were put to death and those who stole vegetables or fruit were punished just like those who committed sacrilege or murder. That is why it was said that Draco wrote his laws in blood, not ink.'

Then, in 593 BC, a nobleman called Solon set up an 'ekklesia' (assembly). This new assembly could make laws, elect officials, and banish anyone it did not trust. This meant Athens was now a democracy, ruled by the people.

After 443 BC, the leading citizen of Athens was a man named Pericles. He was a brilliant speaker and a patron of the arts. It was Pericles who commissioned Phidias to carve the famous Parthenon sculptures. Under his leadership, Athens became a great trading power and built up an EMPIRE.

This illustration comes from a 13th century AD Turkish manuscript and shows Solon in discussion with students.

Source – Plutarch, Life of Solon, 75 AD

Words to use in your project

| empire (group of states under one authority) | orator (public speaker) | vote (means by which someone expresses their political opinion) |
| merciless (showing no mercy) | training (learning, or teaching somebody a skill) | |

SPARTA

The city of Sparta was a breeding ground for the Spartan army. Spartan girls were trained in **ATHLETICS**, so they could grow strong and have strong children. Boys were encouraged to **STEAL**, lie and cheat although they were beaten if they got caught. Plutarch wrote that the Spartan boys:

'... take great care over their stealing, as is shown in the story of one who had stolen a fox cub and had it hidden under his cloak. He endured having his stomach torn by the beast's claws and teeth, and died rather than be detected.'

At the age of seven, all boys were sent to train as soldiers and they had no other education or life besides. Spartan men married at about age 20, but they had to slip away from the barracks secretly at night to visit their wives. Spartan men were not allowed to look at their elders, or show pain or fear. A Spartan mother would kill her son if he was a coward.

This bronze statuette of a woman exercising is from about 520–500 BC.

Source – Plutarch, Life of Lykourgus, 75 AD

The City States Glossary

assembly	Group of people gathered together to make laws		are involved in making decisions and laws
barracks	Place where soldiers live	draconian	Especially harsh or cruel
citizen	A person who actively participates in a society	ostracism	Ignoring people
		Parthenon	Temple built on the Acropolis in Athens in 447–432 BC
commissioned	Somebody given the authority to perform a particular task or duty	polis	A Greek city state
		society	The people in a community and how they are organised
democracy	System where the people		

See also: Ancient Greece 4–5; Wars of the Greeks 8–9; Economy and Society 18–19; Education 22–23

CASE STUDY

This ceramic ostrakhon features the name of Aristeides, from 472 BC.

Ostraka

Each year, Athenians scratched onto pieces of broken pottery called ostraka the name of anyone they thought was becoming too powerful. Then they dropped the ostraka into a box in the marketplace. The man who received the most votes would then be **BANISHED** for 10 years! It was the Athenian way of making sure that no one grew powerful enough to destroy their democracy. We still use the word 'ostracism' to mean ignoring people because we disapprove of them. Sometimes the wording on the ostraka expressed very strong **DISLIKE** of a person. For example, a 5th century BC ostrakon found in the Athenian Agora says:

'This ostrakon says that Aristeides, son of Ariphron is the worst of our accursed leaders.'

Source – Ostraka, 5th century BC

Wars of the Greeks

Greek city states such as Athens and Sparta often fought among themselves, but the Greeks' great foreign ENEMY was Persia. Greece and Persia clashed in a series of wars during the 5th century BC. Greek armies were quite small by today's standards. An army of 10,000 men would be regarded as huge. Although the Greeks were continually at war, large BATTLES were rare – most warfare consisted of marching through enemy territory destroying their crops.

WARRIORS

The best Greek WARRIORS were the hoplites. They wore helmets, breastplates and shin guards of bronze, and carried shields.

Their main **WEAPON** was the spear, but they had swords to use if needed. They fought in long lines, usually eight ranks deep, and each man used his **SHIELD** to protect the right side of the man to his left. A regiment of hoplites was called a 'phalanx', and they would advance to try and drive back the enemy. Some historians think that much

An image of hoplites in formation appears here on a 7th century BC Greek jug.

of a Greek battle consisted simply of trying to push the other side from the field. The best hoplites were the Spartan soldiers. Brilliantly trained, they sang songs and combed their hair before battle. With crimson uniforms, plumed helmets and brightly-polished shields, they marched in short, disciplined steps to the sound of the war-pipes. This must have made the Spartan army a **TERRIFYING** sight. The writer Herodotus described an impression of the Spartan hoplites:

'Be sure, oh King ... that if you can subdue the Spartans, there is no other nation in all the world which will attempt to lift a hand.' (1)

The bravery of the Spartans was noted by the soldier and poet Tyrtaeus:

'It is a fine thing for a brave man to die when he has fallen among the front ranks while fighting for his homeland ... Make the spirit in your heart strong and valiant, and do not be in love with life when you are a fighting man.' (2)

Source – Herodotus, Histories, Book II, 5th century BC (1); Tyrtaeus, The Spartan Creed, 7th century BC (2)

THE NAVY

The Greek warship, the 'trireme', is shown with nine naked oarsmen in this 5th century bc relief from Simonides.

Athenian power depended on the **NAVY**. The city had 200 heavy warboats called 'triremes'. Each ship had 170 rowers and a ramming head at the front. Rowed at full speed into the side of an enemy ship, a trireme could split it in two. In 480 BC the Greek triremes, under the leadership of the Athenians, destroyed the Persian fleet at the battle of Salamis. This Athenian **VICTORY** poem was written about the battle of Salamis:

'The glory of these men's valour will always be undying, For both as foot soldiers and in quick-sailing ships they prevented All Greece from seeing the day of slavery.'

Source – Simonides, Athenian victory poem for the battle of Salamis, 470s BC

Wars of the Greeks Glossary

commemorate	Honour the memory of		26 miles, 385 yards
herald	Person who carries official messages	**Persia**	Country of south-west Asia, now called Iran
hoplites	Heavily armoured Greek warriors	**triremes**	Warships rowed by three banks of oarsmen
Marathon	A place in Greece which gives its name to a running race of exactly	**territory**	Area of land defended by one side against another
		valour	Courage

See also: The City States 6–7; Alexander the Great 10–11; Significant Individuals 14–15; The Olympic Games 28–29

CASE STUDY

The Battle of Marathon

In 490 BC the Persian king, Darius I, tried to conquer Greece with an army of 100,000 men. They were defeated at a place called **MARATHON** by a much smaller army led by General Miltiades. But this battle is more famous for the deeds of the Athenian runner Pheidippides, who was told to run 145 miles to Sparta to ask for help. The writer Herodotus recorded this:

'And first, before they left the city, the generals sent off to Sparta a herald, one Pheidippides, who was by birth an Athenian, and by profession and practice a trained runner ...'

When Sparta refused, Pheidippides ran back to Marathon to tell the army, completing the round trip in two days. The modern marathon distance is based on an additional run that Pheidippides actually never made. Later myths around him said that, after the battle, he ran to Athens to report the Athenian victory, then collapsed and died.

This relief from about 500 BC depicts Pheidippides on his famous run at Marathon.

Source – Herodotus, Histories Book II, 5th century BC

Alexander the Great

Although Sparta defeated Athens in the wars of 431–404 BC, it was not long before the states of Greece united to defeat the Spartans. After 356 BC the states of Greece went to war again. While the states of Greece were ruining and exhausting themselves, King Philip of Macedon was growing more powerful. Philip had a crooked back, a limp and only one eye – but he was a brilliant SOLDIER. In 337 BC he invaded Greece, defeated the Greek armies and declared himself leader of 'the Greeks'.

ALEXANDER THE GREAT'S YOUTH

Alexander, Philip's son, was BRAVE and ambitious. One story describes how at the age of 12, he tamed a wild horse that the best horse-trainers could not control – the horse was called Bucephalus, and it became Alexander's horse until it died.

At age 18, Alexander became commander of the Macedonian cavalry. The Macedonians used cavalry in battle in a new way. Foot soldiers held the enemy back, while the cavalry rode round and attacked them from behind (this is called 'outflanking' the enemy). It made the armies of Macedon undefeatable. In 336 BC, Philip was killed, and Alexander became king. The historian Diodorus described the scene leading up to Philip's death:

'Every seat in the theatre was taken when Philip appeared wearing a white cloak, and by his express orders his **BODYGUARD** held away from him and hollowed only at a distance, since he wanted to show publicly that he was protected by the goodwill of all the Greeks, and had no need of bodyguards.'

This ancient Roman replica of a portrait statue of Alexander the Great is by Lysippos.

Source – Diodorus, Bibliotheca Historica, Book 16, 1st century BC

Words to use in your project

conquer *(to overcome an enemy)*	**knowledge** *(facts or intelligence about something)*	**tactics** *(the plans of carrying out a military operation)*
invasion *(entry of hostile army into a country)*	**slaughter** *(killing of many people)*	**usurp** *(seize power)*

ALEXANDER CONQUERS AN EMPIRE

This 2nd century BC limestone relief shows a scene from the battle between Alexander the Great and King Darius.

In 331 BC Alexander defeated Darius, the Persian king, at the battle of Gaugamela in what is now the country of Iraq. Alexander marched into the Persian capital city of Persepolis and sat on the royal throne. 'So this is what it feels like to be an **EMPEROR!**' he said. For the next five years Alexander marched through the Middle East. But, when he reached India, his men refused to go any further. He had to turn back towards Greece.

In 323 BC he fell ill – probably of malaria, although some believe he was **POISONED** – and died. Alexander's ambitions were recorded by the historian Arrian:

'Alexander's plans had nothing small or mean about them. He would not have been able to remain satisfied with his conquests so far, not even if he had added Europe to Asia and the British Isle to Europe. He would always have been seeking out some unknown land, attempting to rival himself if not anybody else.'

Source – Arrian, The Campaigns of Alexander, Book 7, 2nd century AD

Alexander the Great Glossary

astronomer	Person who studies stars and planets	**museum**	A centre of learning and research
cavalry	Soldiers on horseback	**outflanking**	Getting around the sides of an enemy force and attacking them from behind
circumference	The distance around the outside of a circle or sphere		
malaria	Fever spread by mosquitos	**replica**	Exact copy of an original

See also: The City States 6–7; Wars of the Greeks 8–9; Economy and Society 18–19

CASE STUDY

Alexandria and Hellenism

After Alexander died, the Greeks **RULED** the Middle East for the next two centuries. The city of Alexandria in Egypt became a centre of learning, famous for its library and museum. There, the Greek astronomer Hipparchus calculated the exact length of the year, and the Greek scientist Eratosthenes calculated the circumference of the earth. The people of Alexandria built a lighthouse on the offshore island of Pharos so famous that the modern French word for **LIGHTHOUSE** is 'phare'. Strabo, writing in the 1st century BC, describes the Pharos of Alexandria:

'On top of the island there is a tower magnificently built of white stone, several storeys high, which bears the same name as the island. This was dedicated for the safety of the sailors.'

This Roman bronze coin comes from Pharos island, near Alexandria in Egypt.

Source – Strabo, Geography, 1st century BC

Important Places

Ancient Greece had many great BUILDINGS. Most cities had an 'agora' where markets and government meetings were held. Many also had an acropolis, where temples stood and citizens sheltered in times of enemy attack. Some Greek cities were designed by city planners like Hippodamus. These cities had streets laid out in a grid pattern, rows of identical houses and a large central square.

SANCTUARIES

The ancient Greek cities had large areas for worshipping the gods.

These places were called 'sanctuaries' and were amongst the most spectacular MONUMENTS of the ancient world. They had temples dedicated to the gods and goddesses and altars where sacrifices were performed. One such sanctuary was Delphi. At Delphi you can see the ruins of a temple to the god Apollo. Greeks would go there to find out their future. They would go into a cavern below the temple, where a priestess called the Pythia would go into a drug-induced TRANCE. The priests of Apollo would translate her screams and shouts into a prophecy for the visitor. Many people 'consulted the oracle' – from ordinary farmers to Roman emperors. According to the legend, Alexander the Great did so before he invaded Persia and was told: 'You are invincible'. Xenophon, a writer and a general of the 4th century, describes 'the oracle':

'Socrates advised Xenophon to go to Delphi and consult Apollo. So Xenophon went and asked Apollo to what one of the gods he should sacrifice and pray in order best and most successfully to perform the journey which he had in mind; Apollo in his response told him to what gods he must sacrifice.'

This Greek vase fragment shows people consulting the god Apollo at Delphi, 4th century BC.

Source – Xenophon, The History of My Times, 4th century BC

Words to use in your project

archaeology (study of history through digging up objects)
imposing (impressive in
appearance)
influential (a lasting effect)
ruinous (something in a
ruined state)
sacred (holy)
sacrosanct (most sacred object)

THE AGORA

These small, circular tokens were used for voting purposes in ancient Greece.

'But the most enjoyable thing of all these, which I had forgotten, is when I come home with my pay, and everyone joins in welcoming me back for my money.'

All round the agora were covered walkways, including the Royal Stoa where the laws of Athens were carved into the stones, and the Painted Stoa, where the history of Athens was painted on the walls.

The agora was the busy centre of the city. In Athens, the law courts were held in the agora so it was always packed with old men with no **EMPLOYMENT** who were desperate to be hired as jurors. The famous Athenian comedy writer, Aristophanes described the delights of being paid for being a jury member:

Source – Aristophanes, The Wasps, 5th century BC

Important Places Glossary

agora	Place of assembly or a marketplace		of people chosen to make a judgement in a court of law
altars	Table on which religious offerings are made	**sanctuary**	A holy place like a temple
		sacrifice	The slaughter of an animal or person as an offering to a god
cavern	Large cave		
fortress	Military defence	**temple**	Building devoted to worship of a god
invincible	Too powerful to be defeated		
juror	A member of a jury, a group	**trance**	Sleep-like state

See also: The City States 6–7; Greek Religion 16–17; Economy and Society 18–19; Art and Architecture 24–25

CASE STUDY

This photograph shows the Parthenon, on top of the Acropolis, as it is today.

The Acropolis

Originally a fortress, the **ACROPOLIS** was eventually developed into a place of worship to Athene, the goddess of Athens. The most famous building on the Acropolis is the Parthenon. Another important monument on the Acropolis is the temple of Athene Nike. According to a Greek legend, the king Aegeus was forced to send his son Theseus as a sacrifice to the minotaur, a fierce bull-**MONSTER**. Theseus promised to kill the minotaur saying that he would rig white sails on the returning ships as a sign of his success. Theseus did kill the minotaur, but forgot to change the sails. Seeing the ships and believing his son to be dead, Aegeus was so heartbroken that he threw himself from the Acropolis and was killed. The temple of Athene Nike marks the spot where he stood, looking out to sea, watching for his son. Pausanias, the writer of an ancient travel book about Athens, wrote this about Aegeus:

'From this point in the Acropolis [the temple of Athena Nike] the sea is visible, and here it was that according to legend Aegeus threw himself down to his death.'

Source – Pausanias, Description of Greece, Book 1: Attica, 2nd century AD

Significant Individuals

The Greeks were great thinkers and INVENTORS. They were among the first people to believe that the world could be understood through SCIENCE and mathematics, and were the inventors of democracy. Greece gave birth to many great writers and thinkers who helped to shape the way Greek, and modern society, thought about things. The theories of men such as Pythagoras, Pericles, Homer, Hippocrates, Aristotle and Herodotus are still familiar to students today.

GREAT THINKERS

The most important mathematical figure of the ancient Greek world was Pythagoras. He tried to understand the nature of the gods by studying MATHEMATICS.

Pythagoras discovered important mathematical rules. His discoveries form the basis of modern mathematics, and Pythagoras' theorem about right-angled triangles is still taught in schools today. Pythagoras used his study of mathematics to work out a system of musical scales and chords. The Greek writer Diogenes Laertius described the great man like this:

'His appearance was very dignified, and his students believed that he was Apollo who had come down to earth. There is a story that once, when he was undressing, his legs were made out of gold.'

This marble bust is of the Greek mathematician Pythagoras (c. 580–500 BC).

Source – Diogenes Laertius, The Life of Philosophers, 3rd century AD

Words to use in your project

genius *(very clever)*
incarnation *(god in earthly form)*
innovative *(introducing new*

ideas or methods)
inspire *(create a feeling in a person)*

literature *(written works)*
statesman *(person skilled in the affairs of the state)*

GREAT LEADERS

Greek cities had political parties, each with its own leader. One such leader was Pericles. Pericles began what came to be the most impressive building programme of the ancient world, including the building of the **PARTHENON**. Under Pericles' rule, Athens became the most **ADMIRED** city in Greece. The Greek writer, Thucydides praised the leadership of Pericles in his writings:

'Pericles, because of his position, his intelligence and his known integrity, could respect the freedom of the people and at the same time hold them in check. It was he who led them, rather than they who led him, and since he never sought power from any wrong motive, he was under no necessity of flattering them.'

This stone bust of Pericles from the 5th century BC is housed in the Vatican museum in Rome.

Source – Thucydides, The History of the Peloponnesian War, 5th century BC

Significant Individuals Glossary

accomplishment	Something done or achieved	**philosophy**	Use of reason and argument to seek truth and knowledge about life
chord	Group of three or more musical notes played together	**scales**	Arrangement of musical notes going up or down in order of musical pitch
devastation	Ruins and destruction		
dignified	Impressive or worthy of respect		
integrity	Honesty and good intentions	**theorem**	Maths rule that can be proven through reasoning
motive	Reason for acting out		
multitudes	Masses	**thousandfold**	A thousand times over

See also: The City States 6–7; Wars of the Greeks 8–9; Alexander the Great 10–11; Health and Medicine 26–27

CASE STUDY

Homer

Two key Greek poems are attributed to Homer. *The Iliad* tells how Paris (a prince of the city of Troy) won the love of the **BEAUTIFUL** Helen (the wife of Menelaus, King of Sparta). In revenge, Menelaus fought a ten-year war against Troy. The highlight of the poem is the story of the 'Trojan Horse'. This was when the Greeks pretended to go away, leaving a huge wooden **HORSE** as a present to the Trojans. The Trojans took the horse into their city, but it was full of Greek warriors who sneaked out and opened the gates of the city to their army. *The Iliad* begins like this:

'Sing, goddess, the anger of Peleus' son Achilleus and its devastation, which put pains thousandfold upon the Achaeans, hurled in their multitudes to the house of Hades strong souls of heroes, but gave their bodies to be the delicate feasting of dogs, of all birds and the will of Zeus was accomplished.'

This relief of Helen and her husband Menelaus comes from the 6th century BC.

Source – Homer, The Iliad, 8th century BC

Greek Religion

The Greeks believed that the EARTH was born from a world called Chaos, and that it produced the Heavens and the seas. The Greeks believed in the 'dodekatheon', or 'the 12 GODS', human-like beings who lived on Mount Olympus, where they drank nectar and FEASTED on ambrosia. These gods were immortal and could be cruel and vengeful if wronged – at times hurting or even killing human beings.

GODS AND GODDESSES

The Greeks believed in gods that PROTECTED every part of their lives.

The king of the gods was Zeus, and he was believed to be the most powerful of all. He was the ruler of the skies and lord of the thunderstorm. His wife was Hera, the goddess of marriage and family life. The Greeks praised their gods in songs. Here is an extract from one of the earliest songs of this kind:

'Praise Zeus and queenly Hera and bright-eyed Athena, and Apollo, and Artemis, who delights in arrows, and Poseidon the earth-holder who shakes the earth, and Aphrodite.'

This bronze statue is of the Greek god Zeus, king of all the gods.

Main Gods and Goddesses

Aphrodite	*Goddess of love and beauty*	**Demeter**	*Goddess of agriculture*
Apollo	*God of light and purity, poetry and music, healing, and prophecy*	**Hephaistus**	*God of craftsmanship*
		Hera	*Goddess of marriage and wife of Zeus*
Ares	*God of war*	**Hermes**	*God of merchants and messages*
Artemis	*Goddess of hunting and wildlife*	**Hestia**	*Goddess of the family*
		Poseidon	*God of the sea and earthquakes*
Athene	*Goddess of wisdom and war, and goddess of Athens*	**Zeus**	*King of the gods and god of the sky*

Source – Hesiod, Theogony, 7th century BC

HEROES

Greek **HEROES** were mortal men who became superhuman because of their achievements. Some of the most famous heroes include Achilles, a Greek warrior who fought in the Trojan war. Dipped in the magic River Styx at birth, his body was immune to death – every part except his heel, which led to his death when Paris shot a poisoned arrow into it. Orpheus was a poet and musician who went into Hades (hell) to rescue his lover Eurydice when she died, but lost her because he looked behind him when he was warned not to. Perseus became a hero for killing the gorgon, whose

appearance turned men to stone if they looked at it. Theseus became a hero when he killed the Minotaur that lived in a **LABYRINTH** at Knossos:

'When he arrived at Crete ... having a clue of thread given him by Ariadne, who had fallen in love with him, and being instructed by her how to use it so as to conduct him through the windings of the labyrinth, he escaped out of it and slew the Minotaur, and sailed back, taking along with him Ariadne and the young Athenian captives.'

This Athenian cup from about 460 BC has images of Theseus' heroic deeds.

Source – Plutarch, Life of Theseus, 75 AD

Greek Religion Glossary

ambrosia	The food of the gods	labyrinth	Complicated network
Classical	Period relating to the ancient Greeks		of passages or paths
		minotaur	Mythical monster that is half man and half bull
gorgon	Woman with snakes for hair who could turn people to stone	nectar	Sweet syrup produced by flowers
immune	Not affected by something (like diseases)	superhuman	Beyond normal human ability

CASE STUDY

Heracles is shown receiving the Golden Apples of the Hesperides in this relief from the Temple of Zeus, Olympia, 5th century BC.

Heracles

The most famous Greek hero was Heracles, who was also worshipped as a god. Heracles was the son of Zeus and Alkmene. He performed great achievements, called the 'labours', such as **KILLING** monsters that devastated the Greek countryside. One of his labours involved collecting Cerberus, the guard-dog of the Underworld. Heracles was the hero of labour and struggle, protecting men from **BEASTS** and danger. Heracles is often represented as the ideal of manly strength. The Greek writer, Herodotus wrote about Heracles:

'... my own opinion is that the Greeks act most wisely when they build and maintain two temples of Heracles, in the one of which Heracles is worshipped as a god, while in the other the honours paid are such as are due to a hero.'

Source – Herodotus, Histories Book II, 5th century BC

Economy and Society

In 593 BC, the Athenian leader Solon restructured Athenian society. He declared that there were four significant CLASSES at the top there were the nobles; then the 'hippeis' (people who were rich enough to own horses); then the 'zeugitai' (farmers with a plough); and, finally, the 'thetes' (the poorest landowners). Below these classes there were SLAVES, taken from captured lands and sold to wealthy Greeks as servants.

RICH AND POOR

Rich and poor people had very different lifestyles. The rich lived in large town houses, while the poor had much more basic homes.

Many rich people had a **HOUSE** in the **COUNTRY** to escape to if they ever tired of city life. Their mud-brick or stone houses, whitewashed to deflect the heat of the sun, had large rooms and **COURTYARDS**. Their wealth enabled the rich to dress in elegant clothes, made from imported materials such as cotton and silk from India and the East. The rich also kept slaves – mostly abandoned children or foreigners captured in war. Greek slaves were not badly treated and if they saved enough money, they could buy their freedom. Asked when slavery would end, the Greek comedian Crates joked:

'... only when the pots wash themselves, food cooks itself and hot water comes straight from the pipes.'

This relief shows a man accompanied by a child slave, c. 430 BC.

The houses of the poor were made in the same way as those of the rich, but rooms were much smaller, and their homes were packed together. Peasants grew their own food to feed their families, often difficult on the parched Greek soil. Donkeys were used for carrying goods around over the mountainous terrain of Greece, and sometimes even for ploughing fields when the family could not afford an ox.

Source – Crates, Fragment of a now lost comedy, 5th century BC

TRADESMEN AND TRADERS

The Greeks did not just live in Greece. They sailed off and set up settlements (colonies) all over the Mediterranean. Athens depended on imports, and hundreds of **TRADERS** brought in grain, fish, meat and timber from Macedonia, tin from Britain, copper from Cyprus, papyrus from Egypt and spices, dyes, ivory, raisins, apples, figs and slaves from other places. A writer named Hermippus described the wealth and products that were brought in to Athens through international trade:

'From Cyrene silphium and ox hides, from the Hellespont mackerel and all kinds of salted fish, from Italy salt and ribs of beef, from Egypt sails and rope, from Syria frankincense, from Crete cypress for the gods, Libya provides abundant ivory to buy, Rhodes, raisins and sweet figs, but from Euboea pears and fat apples. Slaves from Phrygia, Paphlagonia provides dates and oily almonds.'

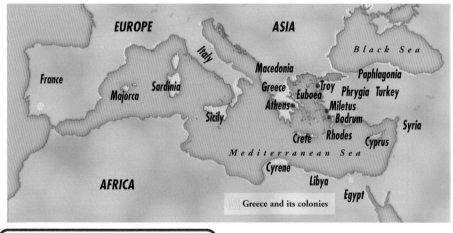

Greece and its colonies

EUROPE — ASIA — France — Italy — Majorca — Sardinia — Macedonia — Greece — Euboea — Troy — Phrygia — Turkey — Athens — Miletus — Bodrum — Sicily — Crete — Rhodes — Syria — Cyprus — Cyrene — Libya — Egypt — AFRICA — Black Sea — Mediterranean Sea

Source – Hermippus, Phormophoroi, 5th century BC

Economy and Society Glossary

class	A level or rank in society
colonies	Settlements controlled by another country
Cyrene	Ancient Greek city in North Africa
Euboea	Greek island
Hellespont	Old name for the Dardanelles, a narrow passage of water

	linking Europe to Turkey
heroine	Main female character
imports	Goods traded into a country
Paphlagonia	Ancient region of northern Asia
slave	A person kept for free or cheap labour
terrain	Land

See also: Ancient Greece 4–5; The City States 6–7; Important Places 12–13; Education 22–23

CASE STUDY

Women

WOMEN were not highly valued in Greek society. Greek mothers wanted boy children, and girl babies were often thrown out to die. Girls were not sent to school – they were taught to do household jobs such as spinning and cooking. While it was common for an Athenian man to marry at about age 30, most girls married as young as 15. Women were not allowed to leave the **HOUSEHOLD**, and were expected to run to the 'gunaikeion' (women's room) if they even met a male visitor in the courtyard. Lysistrata, the heroine in an ancient Greek play, described the life of Athenian women:

'It's difficult for women to get out of the house. For one will be running around for her husband, another waking up a slave, or with the baby, putting it to bed, or washing it or feeding it.'

This marble woman's head dates from around 350 BC, and comes from the Temple of Athena, Polias.

Source – Aristophanes, Lysistrata, 5th century BC

Food and Farming

The Greeks ate a wide variety of food, thanks to the fortunate position of their country in the middle of the Mediterranean Sea. The wealthy ate very well, while the poor had a far more limited DIET, supplemented with food grown on their own land. Many also kept ANIMALS for milk and food. The Greek climate was perfect for farming, with mild winters and hot, sunny summers. As a result, the people were able to raise CROPS all year round.

GREEK DIET

The staple food for ancient Greeks was a kind of bread made from wheat or barley flour.

This was often soaked in olive oil at breakfast and eaten with fruit. The Greeks also grew and ate a wide selection of vegetables. These included peas, garlic, lettuce, parsley, onions, mushrooms, artichokes, beets and cucumbers. Meat was not often eaten by the poor outside religious festivals, but boar, deer and rabbit were regular additions to the dining tables of the rich. **SEAFOOD** was eaten more widely. It was much more affordable, as the Mediterranean Sea that surrounds Greece provided its people with a plentiful source of food. Greeks of all classes drank **WINE**, which was thick and usually diluted to taste. Greeks believed that the harvest was determined by the mood of the gods, and that living an honest life would lead to bountiful crops. The writer Hesiod expressed this view:

'The earth bears them victual in plenty, and on the mountains the oak bears acorns upon the top and bees in the midst. Their woolly sheep are laden with fleeces; their women bear children like their parents. They flourish continually with good things, and do not travel on ships, for the grain-giving earth bears them fruit.'

This Greek vase shows a man ladling wine from krater to cup, 6th century BC.

Source – Hesiod, Works and Days, 7th century BC

Words to use in your project

agriculture *(farming)*
barley *(hardy cereal)*
celestial *(to do with the stars)*

harvest *(process of gathering in crops)*
reap *(cut or gather crop)*

seasonal *(lasting for a season)*
supplement *(something added)*
temperate *(mild climate)*

FARMING

This model of a man using a plough drawn by two oxen is from the 7th–6th century BC.

In the spring, the **FARMERS** tended grape and olive groves. These were harvested in Autumn. Also, the wheat and barley crops were planted in Autumn, and harvested in the Spring. The main animal that was raised on the farms was the **PIG**.

'First of all, get a house, and a woman and an ox for the plough – a slave woman and not a wife, to follow the oxen as well – and make everything ready at home, so that you may not have to ask of another, and he refuses you, and so, because you are in lack, the season pass by and your work come to nothing. Do not put your work off till tomorrow and the day after; for a sluggish worker does not fill his barn, nor one who puts off his work: industry makes work go well, but a man who puts off work is always at hand-grips with ruin.'

| Source – Hesiod, Works and Days, 7th century BC |

Food and Farming Glossary

astrolabe	A device for reading the movements of the stars and planets	**crop**	Plants grown for food
		fleece	A sheep's woollen coat
		flourish	Healthy development
astrology	Study of how the movements of the stars affect people	**krater**	Large bowl
		Pleiades	A star cluster near Orion
barley	A grain used for food	**sickle**	Farming tool with blade use for cutting crops
bountiful	Very large or generous		

CASE STUDY

This illustration from a 13th century manuscript shows the mathematicians Euclid and Herman Dalmatin trying to read the skies using a piece of primitive equipment called an astrolabe.

Astrology and Food

Some Greeks thought farming was controlled by the movement of the **STARS** in the skies. This view was expressed by Hesiod:

'When the Pleiades, daughters of Atlas, are rising, begin your harvest, and your ploughing when they are going to set. Forty nights and days they are hidden and appear again as the year moves round, when first you sharpen your sickle. This is the law of the plains, and of those who live near the sea, and who inhabit rich country, the glens and dingles far from the tossing sea, – strip to sow and strip to plough and strip to reap, if you wish to get in all Demeter's fruits in due season, and that each kind may grow in its season.'

| Source – Hesiod, Works and Days, 7th century BC |

Education

In the early period of ancient Greece, few people could READ or WRITE. Information was passed on in other ways. One way was through the poetry of Homer, which taught people about history and the principles they were expected to live by. People learned by memorising information. From about 750 BC, however, the ancient Greek ALPHABET began to be used. Only the children of rich families went to school.

WRITING

The Greeks did not invent writing, but they were the first people to develop letters for VOWEL sounds.

With the development of their own language, the Greeks became the first society where large numbers of people could read. Surprisingly, many Greeks did not like book-learning. The Greek philosopher Plato thought that it ruined the **MEMORY** and dragged the reader away from what was happening in the real world. The Greek writer, Herodotus, described how the Greeks took the alphabet from the Phoenicians and adapted it to create their own alphabet:

'Originally the Greeks shaped their letters exactly like the Phoenicians, but afterwards in the course of time, they changed the alphabet and the shape of the letters.'

Funerary stone inscribed with the name of the dead, Kleomoiris, 1st century BC, from the eastern necropolis of Filippi.

Source – Histories Book II, by Herodotus, 5th century BC

Words to use in your project

argument (exchange of views)
astronomy (study of Space and the Universe)
learned (great knowledge achieved through study)
logic (science of reasoning)
proverb (short saying meant to state a general truth)
verse (poetry)

SCHOOL

This Illustration from a 13th century Turkish manuscript features the Greek philosopher Aristotle with his students.

Athenian boys went to **SCHOOL** between the ages of 7 and 14. At first, they learned reading, writing and mathematics, and spent a lot of time trying to memorise the poems of Homer. As they grew older, they studied other subjects like astronomy, geography, history and rhetoric (**PUBLIC SPEAKING**). They also spent a lot of time doing athletics training. Every pupil had a slave who sat behind him and hit him if he didn't concentrate. A character in a Greek comedy revealed how highly school was thought of:

'Here it is. A logic-factory for the extra-clever. They can teach you to win your arguments, and they are real gentlemen.'

Source – Aristophanes, The Clouds, 5th century BC

Education Glossary

alphabet	A body of letters used in writing	**logic**	Correct reasoning
fable	A made-up story in which animals can speak and which teaches a life lesson	**oxen**	Animal kept for milk or meat, eg: cow or bull
		proverb	A saying which carries good advice for life
funerary	Burial	**phonetic**	The sounds of letters
legendary	Famous/based on stories	**rhetoric**	Formal speech

See also: Ancient Greece 4–5; Significant Individuals 14–15; Economy and Society 18–19; Theatre 30–31

CASE STUDY

Aesop's Fables

Aesop was a Greek slave. His fables were another way people could learn wisdom without having to read it in a book. They are short **STORIES** with a moral. They come from the time of Homer and there are more than 650 of them. The most famous is probably the story of the tortoise and the hare, which reminded people that it is better to work carefully and slowly than carelessly and quickly. Here is an example of a fable called 'The Four Oxen and the Lion':

'A Lion used to prowl about a field in which Four Oxen lived, but, when he tried to attack them; they stood tail-to-tail and he was met by the horns of one of them whichever way he approached. One day, however, the oxen quarrelled, and each went off to graze alone in a separate corner of the field. Then the Lion attacked them one by one and soon he had eaten all four.'

A medieval illustration of Aesop, the legendary Greek author of a collection of fables.

Source – Aesop, Fables, 7th century BC

Art and Architecture

The Athenians tried to make their art and architecture as beautiful as possible. Their style of architecture was based on EGYPTIAN examples, using tall columns to create grand civic buildings. Buildings were often decorated with SCULPTURES that reflected their great talent at stonemasonry. The Greeks were also great artists, and many of their wall paintings and pottery survive today. Artists illustrated scenes from stories or from everyday life.

GREEK COLUMNS

Greek architects built their public buildings using COLUMNS and beams.

At first the columns were very strong and thick – these are called 'Doric' columns. As time went on, however, Greek architects learned how to make the columns more slender ('Ionic') and ornate ('Corinthian'). Greek architecture was copied by the Romans and, later, by the Victorians. An ancient writer described the complexity of Greek architecture:

'... the temples of Athena, Ares, and Heracles, will be Doric, since the virile strength of these gods makes daintiness entirely inappropriate to their houses. In temples to Aphrodite, Spring-Water, and the Nymphs, the Corinthian order will be found to have peculiar significance, because these are delicate divinities and so its rather slender outlines, its flowers, leaves, and ornamental volutes will lend propriety where it is due. The construction of temples of the Ionic order to Hera, Artemis, Bacchus, and the other gods of that kind, will be in keeping with the middle position which they hold; for the building of such will be an appropriate combination of the severity of the Doric and the delicacy of the Corinthian.'

The terms of the truce called during each Olympic Games were engraved on a truce discus and kept at this temple of Hera at Olympia.

Source – Vitruvius, On Architecture, 1st century BC

Words to use in your project

amphorae *(Greek vessel with two handles and a narrow neck)*

construction *(the act of building something)*
legacy *(lasting influence)*

realistic *(showing life as it is)*
treasury *(place or building where treasure is stored)*

PAINTING AND SCULPTURE

This scene from the Parthenon frieze shows oxen being taken for sacrifice.

Many Greek buildings were covered with fine frescoes, friezes and **PAINTINGS**. Not only were these pieces of art very beautiful, but they often illustrated important events in ancient Greece. One frieze from the Parthenon illustrates the Panathenaic Festival, a very important occasion in the lives of Athenians. The frieze shows a procession on the way to the Parthenon – with **CHARIOTS**, musicians, maidens and victims due to be sacrificed being carried out there. Cows and sheep are being taken to the sacrifice too, and people carry trays of food and fine wines. The frieze was carved out of **MARBLE**, but it was also painted with lively colours like blue, red and gold.

CASE STUDY

The Parthenon

The Parthenon was a Doric **TEMPLE** dedicated to the goddess Athene, although it was used more as a storage place for the city treasury than as a place of worship. It took ten years to build, and was finished in 438 BC. Inside, the building would have been very dark, as no light came in apart from through the doorway. In later times, the Parthenon was used as a Christian church and a Turkish mosque, and then as a gunpowder store. Eventually it was left to fall into **RUINS**. Plutarch wrote:

'... what brought most pleasure and adornment in Athens, most startled other men, and is the only evidence about Athens' power and prosperity was the erection of sacred buildings, like the Parthenon.'

The great Greek sculptor Phidias carved a gold and ivory statue of Athene, to be kept inside the Parthenon, which had his name inscribed upon it.

The Parthenon was built on the Acropolis at Athens between 447–432 BC.

Art and Architecture Glossary

architecture	Designing buildings		applied to fresh plaster
civic	Related to a city	**frieze**	Long strip of sculpture or painting on a wall
complexity	Difficult to understand because of the many different parts	**inscribed**	Carved words
		monument	Building erected to honour something or someone
Corinthian	Relating to Corinth – a city state in ancient Greece	**mosque**	Muslim place of worship
divinities	Gods and goddesses	**propriety**	Correct behaviour
frescoes	Painting when watercolour is	**virile**	Strong and energetic

See also: Important Places 12–13; Greek Religion 16–17; Economy and Society 18–19; The Olympic Games 28–29

Source – Plutarch, Life of Pericles, 75 AD

Health and Medicine

Like the Egyptians, the Greeks were very interested in the workings of the human body. Greek DOCTORS believed that the function of each part of the body was critical to good health. Basic OPERATIONS were carried out by physicians. Health and medicine were heavily influenced by religion, and offerings were made to the gods in an attempt to aid recovery.

GREEK DOCTORS

Greek philosophers believed that the BODY was made up of four 'humours' – black bile, phlegm, blood and yellow bile.

Greek doctors took these ideas and developed them into a theory of health based on the idea of balancing opposites. They believed that when the four humours were in balance, a person would be healthy. Doctors were looked up to and expected to be of immaculate appearance, as shown by this extract from a Greek text:

'The position of a doctor must make him careful to keep his complexion and weight at their correct standard ... He must have a clean appearance, and wear good clothes, using a sweet-smelling scent ... In facial expression he should be controlled but not grim. For grimness seems to indicate harshness and a hatred of mankind, while a man who bursts into guffaws and is too cheerful is considered vulgar.'

The ruins of the Asklepion hospital and medical school on the island of Kos, where Hippocrates once taught.

Source – Hippocrates, The Physician, 320 BC

MIRACLE CURES

For HOSPITALS the Greeks used the sanctuaries to the god of healing Asclepios, called the Asclepieia.

They believed the god came to help them as they slept. As time went on, most Asclepieia became **HEALTH RESORTS**, with guest houses and a stadium and swimming pool where patients could exercise and recuperate. There are many stories of miraculous **CURES** at the Asclepieia, including this inscription at the sanctuary of Asclepius at Epidauros:

This tombstone of the doctor, Claudius Agathemorus, and his wife comes from Rome, late 1st century.

'Cleo was pregnant for five years. After the fifth year of pregnancy, she came as a supplant to the god and slept in the Abaton. As soon as she had left it and was outside the sacred area, she gave birth to a son who, as soon as he was born, washed himself at the fountain and walked about with his mother. After this success, she inscribed upon an offering: "The wonder is not the size of the inscription, but the act of the god: Cleo bore a burden in her stomach for five years, until she slept here and the god made her well."'

Source – Inscription from the Asclepieion at Epidauros, 3rd century BC

Health and Medicine Glossary

bile	Fluid secreted in the liver	immaculate	Perfectly clean and tidy
characterised	Way something made itself known	phlegm	Mucus created in the nose or airways of the body
clinical	Treatment of patients	recuperate	To recover from an illness
diagnosis	Working out the nature of an illness or medical complaint	supplant	Needy person
		vulgar	Lacking class or good taste
guffaws	Loud and lively laughing		

CASE STUDY

A marble bust of Hippocrates, the Greek physician known as the father of medicine.

Hippocrates

Hippocrates was a Greek doctor who lived on the island of Cos in the 5th and 4th centuries BC. He invented the system of diagnosis called 'clinical observation' which forms the basis of modern medicine. Hippocrates is often called the 'Father of Medicine'. Hippocrates popularised the idea of **'NATURAL HEALING'** using opposites. For example, his cure for a cold – which was characterised by phlegm (which was cold and wet) – was to sit the patient by the fire (which was hot and dry). Hippocrates wrote in his main work:

'The chief controlling factors for good health are the weather, the type of country and the sort of water which is drunk.'

Source – Hippocrates, On airs, waters and places, 4th century BC

The Olympic Games

The Greeks believed that by playing COMPETITIVE SPORTS they honoured the gods and the dead. They had four major EVENTS that were held every four years: the Olympian Games and the Nemean Games, both in honour of Zeus, the Pythian Games and the Isthmian Games. The most important and famous games, however, were the Olympian Games.

THE GAMES

The first Olympic Games took place at Olympia near the town of Elis in 776 BC.

The Greeks believed that the hero Heracles was the founder of the Olympian (now known as the Olympic) Games. They were held in summer every four years. People came from all over Greece and, for the month before the games, wars stopped so that people could travel there safely. On one occasion, the Spartans were banned from the Games because they would not stop **FIGHTING**. In revenge, the Spartans attacked Elis, but even they dared not stop the Games. It is thought that 20,000 competitors went to the Games. But the Games were for men only – women, foreigners and slaves were not allowed to enter the holy area of the Games. **ATHLETES** who won a prize at the Games became very famous. Although all they were given was a simple laurel wreath, when they got home they were heroes. They never had to pay taxes again and were given free meals for the rest of their life. Pausanias, writing in the 2nd century AD, in his book *Periegesis*, tells us just how highly the Games were spoken of:

'Many are the sights to be seen in Greece, and many are the wonders to be heard; but on nothing does Heaven bestow more care than the Olympic Games.'

This statue of a Greek discus thrower dates from around the 3rd century AD.

Source – Pausanias, Periegesis, 2nd century AD

THE SANCTUARY

The Olympic Games took place in the sanctuary of Zeus at Olympia. It is important to remember that the Olympic Games were not just a sports event, but a 5-day **RELIGIOUS FESTIVAL** to the god Zeus. Much of the Olympic site has survived, and was excavated by German archaeologists in the 19th century. This included the Prytaneion, where the winners of the Olympic Games were served feasts. The altar of Hestia was also located here – where the eternal **FLAME** for the Olympic Games burned. Pausanias, writing in the 2nd century AD, gives a description of the layout of the complex:

Some of the Sanctuary of Zeus at Olympia is still standing today. Here are the ruins of the temple of Hera.

'The Eleans also have a banqueting room. This too is in the Prytaneion, opposite the chamber where stands the hearth. In this room they entertain the winners in the Olympic Games.'

Source – Pausanias, The Periegesis, 2nd century AD

CASE STUDY

An Olympic Victor

Diagoras of Rhodes was probably the most famous **BOXER** in the ancient world. He won competitions in all four major games (Olympic, Pythian, Nemean and Isthmian) in 464 BC, while three of his sons and two of his grandsons were Olympic victors. His statue stood at Olympia. When his sons won in the Olympic games, they carried him through the crowd, while the Greeks threw flowers and congratulated him and his sons. Diagoras was honoured by all Greeks and the famous fifth-century poet Pindar wrote a poem celebrating his victories:

'O father Zeus, honour the hymn for an Olympic victory and the man who has won success at boxing, and grant him respectful favour from both his own townsmen and foreigners.'

This statue of a boxer was made in the 1st century BC by Apollonius.

The Olympic Games Glossary

ampitheatre	Round, unroofed building with seats surrounding a central area		goes out
		excavated	Object dug up by for studying history
chamber	Large room used for special events	**festival**	Day or period of celebration, often religious
complex	Group of buildings		
eternal flame	The flame which never	**laurel**	Leaves from the bay tree

See also: The City States 6–7; Wars of the Greeks 8–9; Important Places 12–13; Greek Religion 16–17

Source – Pindar, Olympic poems, 5th century BC

Theatre

The Greeks invented theatre. Festivals developed out of a religious cult which worshipped Dionysus, the god of wine. Part of the ceremony was the 'dithyramb' – a chant sung and danced by a CHORUS of men. During the 6th century BC, a Greek called Thespis added an actor who spoke to the chorus – our modern word 'thespian' comes from his name. As time went on, a second and a third actor were added, and the chorus was reduced to 12–15 men.

TRAGEDY

In 534 BC, the people of Athens turned the festivals of Dionysus into a competition held twice a year (in January and March).

In each of the festivals theatrical plays would be performed and the Athenian **AUDIENCE** would vote for the best one, which would then win a prize. **TRAGEDY** was the most highly esteemed form of theatre play. The word tragedy comes from two Greek words: 'tragos' (goat – probably a reference to the goat which was sacrificed during the festival) and 'ode' (song). Five competitors had to write three tragedies and a shorter, less serious play called a 'satyricon' (from which we get our modern word 'satire'). Tragedies usually took stories from the Greek **MYTHS**, and were about great heroes refusing to accept their fate, usually with disastrous results (which gives us our modern meaning of the word 'tragedy'). This excerpt below gives a flavour of a typical Greek tragedy:

'Unwept, without friends, without marriage-song, I am led in misery on this journey that cannot be put off. No longer is it permitted me, unhappy girl, to look up at this sacred eye of the burning sun. But for my fate no tear is shed, no friend moans in sorrow.'

The ancient theatre of Dionysis lies on the southern slope of the Acropolis in Athens.

Source – Sophocles, Antigone, 5th century BC

Words to use in your project

act (main division of a play or opera)
acoustics (quality of sound in a place)
epilogue (end of a play)
interlude (pause between acts of a play)
prologue (speech or poem introducing a play)

COMEDY

After 487 BC, the first comedies were introduced into the festivals of Dionysus. Five competitors wrote one play each. The greatest **COMEDY** playwright was Aristophanes. The comedies were often crazy **FANTASIES** – such as Aristophanes' *Birds*, where the hero builds a city in the sky called Cloud-cuckoo-land – and the playwrights put in anything they thought would get a laugh. Aristophanes' plays are full of **RUDE** scenes, and he poked fun at everybody, especially public figures like Pericles. Aristophanes claims he is offering valuable advice to the Athenians, in his 5th century play *The Acharnians*:

'But now, O People, give me your attention, if you love the truth, for the poet would now like to criticize his audience.'

This bust features the two Greek playwrights Sophocles and Aristophanes, 4th century BC.

Source – Aristophanes, The Acharnians, 5th century BC

Theatre Glossary

audience	Assembled spectators at an event	**playwright**	A person who writes plays
chorus	A group of performers who comment together on the main action of a play	**satire**	Use of ridicule to expose shortcomiings or failures
		thespian	An actor or actress, or a term used to relate to tragedy or drama
comedy	A play with an amusing theme, looking at everyday situations	**tragedy**	A play dealing with tragic events

See also: Ancient Greece 4–5; Wars of the Greeks 8–9; Greek Religion 16–17; Education 22–23

CASE STUDY

Actors

In Greece, only men were **ACTORS**. They wore huge masks, bright clothes and shoes with high heels to make them big enough to be seen from the back of the theatre. They probably over-acted terribly. If the audience did not like the play, they would throw fruit and even stones, so it was dangerous being an actor.

This Greek statue of an actor, comes from the 2nd century BC.

Index

GREEK TIMELINE

3,000–1,500 BC
Minoan culture appears on the island of Crete.

2,000–1,700 BC
Large-scale invasions of Greek-speaking peoples into mainland Greece.

1,700–1,100 BC
Mycenaean development (under Minoan influence), peak and decline (after 1,250 BC) of Mycenaean culture in mainland Greece.

1,100–850 BC
Break-up of Mycenaean civilisation; Greek settlements throughout the Aegean Islands and the coast of Asia Minor.

850–480 BC
Redevelopment of overseas trade. Alphabetic script introduced, 750 BC. Emergence of Greek city states.

480–323 BC
Greek city states thrive until overshadowed by the powerful Macedonian kings.

323–146 BC Hellenistic Period.
Alexander's empire fragments into Greek monarchies in Macedonia, Syria and Egypt.

Roman overseas expansion begins in 208 BC. Greece becomes a Roman province. The Roman Republic ends with a seizure of power by Julius Caesar (assassinated 44 BC).

400–1453 AD Byzantine Period.
After the collapse of the western part of the Roman Empire around 476 AD, Greece continued to be ruled by Romans, but now from their new capital at Constantinople.

In 1453 AD Greece was taken over by the Turks and became part of the Ottoman Empire.

PICTURE CREDITS: Alamy: 26b, 29c. **Ancient Art and Architecture:** 30b. **Art Archive:** 5tl, 5tr, 6b, 7tl, 7tr, 8b, 9tl, 9br, 10b, 11tl, 12b, 14b, 15c, 15br, 17c, 17tr, 18c, 19br, 20b, 20-21c, 21tr, 22b, 23t, 23br, 25t, 26-27tc, 27tr, 30-31c. **British Museum:** 11br, 13c, 13tl, 16r, 31r.